Eating Along the Way!

A Survivor's Guide for people who are serious about hearing God's call

By

Evangelist Linda Sweezer

ISBN: 0-7596-8646-7

This book is printed on acid free paper.

1stBooks - rev. 02/01/02

DEDICATION...

I take this grand opportunity to dedicate this book to my best friend the Holy Spirit and to one of his Women of Virtue, Ramona Latham. Ramona has worked tirelessly and diligently with me in getting **Eating Along The Way!** out to the general public. After she read the manuscript, she told me she was ready for me to write **Eating SOME MORE Along The Way!**

For all of the long hours, the late night phone calls, and the great sacrifices, I dedicate my first Holy Ghost book to you. Thank you for every minute that you gave to the Lord through helping me get this work out to the world.

MAY GOD FOREVER BLESS YOU!

Evangelist Sweezer

FOREWORD

My book, **Eating Along The Way!**, was written under the unction of the Holy Spirit. God spoke a word to my current pastor, Reverend Larry A. Nicks, on September 7, 2000, and he challenged me to write down seven topics of my choice and to develop them on paper. On this day, God spoke through him that I needed to write a book. He challenged me to have the topics done before the end of the year. Needless to say, I did get it done, but it was right at the end of the year 2000. I gave it to Pastor Nicks. God spoke through him again two other times and said firmly—write the book now.

I always knew I would one day write a book but I had no idea that God wanted my book written right away! My mother often told me that she would like to see me write a book since the plays that I had written over the years had been so successful.

One of the strongest prophetic words came to me about writing my book just before we took a trip to visit with Dr. Barbara King in Atlanta, Georgia. Pastor Nicks, Reverend Troy Truly, and I were in the conference room of Vicksburg Family

Development Service planning our PowerPoint presentation when all of a sudden the Spirit of God moved upon the Pastor and he began to prophesy to Reverend Truly and to me. The word was so strong that all I could do was cry and said, "Okay, Lord, I'll write the book." I later remembered that God is not looking for our "ability," but for our "availability." When Kay Lee, Pastor Nicks, Reverend Truly, and I went to Atlanta, the Spirit of God awakened me in the middle of the night at 2:00 a.m. and said, "Write this down." I had a pad by my bed (very common for me) and the Holy Ghost gave me **Eating Along The Way!**. I thought it would be the title of the next message that I would preach, but He clearly said, "This is the title of your book." I didn't think about it anymore until I sat down with my paper and pen in hand to begin my book. I had no clue what this title meant until I was actually writing the book. The Holy Ghost "fed" me along the way as I wrote it. The truth of the matter is—this is how every play and every sermon comes—he feeds it to me as I write and I never know the content or the outcome until I'm there. Every sermon that I've ever preached was "fed" to me as I opened my mouth in submission to His holy will. God said this book would change lives, set the captives free, and cause a "stirring" in the ministerial community. He told me there were people "waiting" for this book. I'm only being an obedient servant to write it. Father, here it is, Your book, Your words—let Your will be done!

Amen

"It is so!"

Pastor Evangelist Linda Sweezer

SPECIAL THANKS...

I take this means of thanking those who worked hard in the service of the Lord. Special thanks to my husband, Tony, my children, Anthony and Ann, who all supported me during this time of ministry; Pastor Larry Nicks, Sister Carla Nicks, Reverend Troy Truly and Sister Joan Truly, Reverend Dexter Jones and Sister Deborah Jones, and the Triumph MB Church Family; Pastors Mitchell Dent and Deborah Dent; Minister Kevin Abraham; Ramona Latham; Yolande Robbins; Brother Anderson Jones and Sister Felicia Jones; Felicia Catchings; Michelle Johnson, who encouraged me to keep writing; Kay Lee and the staff of Vicksburg Family Development Service.

CHAPTER ONE

THE CALL

"My name is Lemon" were the most common words I remember saying when I was a child. I couldn't say "Linda," but "Lemon" was the word that instantly came out of my mouth when I was asked what my name was. Little did I know that "Lemon" would have a prophetic meaning for all the hardships I would face as a child.

The neighborhood where I grew up on Locust Street was rich in its quantity of children. We had a basketball goal in the back yard, and all of the children from near and far would come to play with my older brothers and sisters. All of our free time was spent playing hopscotch, marbles, or basketball. As the youngest of ten children, my opportunities for playing basketball were very limited because I always had to wait in line for the ball. There was a giant fig tree in our yard that was my favorite spot to play. It was on the side of our house and was always very fruitful. It was under this tree that I sometimes cried and would feel all alone. I did a lot of pondering about why I was alive under this fig tree. I often wondered, "Why is it I don't fit in with the other children in this neighborhood?" I remember thinking, "Why don't I have a boyfriend like the rest of the girls do—what's wrong with me?" My self-esteem was very low because I didn't like myself at all.

When the Lord called me into the ministry, one of the scriptures He gave me was *John 1:48,* **Nathaniel saith unto him, whence knowest thou me? Jesus answered and saith unto him, Before that Philip called thee, when thou wast under the fig tree, I saw thee**. The Holy Spirit told me about all that ever I did! I knew that only He knew of my tears under my fig tree. Hallelujah! My Lord was listening even when I didn't know it.

Best of all, we lived next to a grocery store that had all kinds of goodies in it. The name of that store was Price's Grocery, and all I ever wanted to do was to get my hands on a dime or a quarter so that I could buy a black cake or a stage plank or a giant dill pickle. A white family who seemed to really like Black people owned the store. The store was small with the ice cream box all the way in the back to the left. The cash register was on the right hand side and sometimes there were a lot of people standing around. It was very common for me to see black and white people talking and smiling with one another.

Mr. Moses' store was up the hill and had an even warmer atmosphere. They had a butcher in the back of this store who would cut us a dollar's worth of bologna, lunchmeat, or salami. That was the best meat I ever had. Mr. Moses was kind to everyone who came into his store and he had a lot of business every day. At this stage in my life, things were pretty typical.

But as far back as I can remember I knew that there was a God. I remember praying to ask Him for things rather than just thanking Him for his goodness. I remember going to church and getting up to recite the Apostles' Creed which I learned in the Catholic pre-school I attended. Can you imagine a small child in the Baptist church regularly reciting the Apostles' Creed in Sunday School?

As you have probably already figured out, I have never been a traditionally thinking person.

But the interesting thing is that the members of Mt. Zion #1 Missionary Baptist Church seemed to love the Apostles' Creed too, and often called on me to recite it on Sundays.

When I look back on all of this, I can see how God had me eating from many tables in order to prepare me for the many diverse denominations to which I would minister. God also knows and is the author of the great love that I have for people of all races, cultures, and backgrounds. **Hereby perceive we the love of God, because he laid down his life for us: and we ought to lay down our lives for the brethren.** *I John 3:16*

As a child, I remember being afraid all the time. My brothers and sisters would always tease me by saying, "The boogie-man's going to get you!" And I believed that this "monster" was real, and consequently had a hard time getting to sleep at night. There was a closet in my bedroom downstairs in our two-story house that had no door on it. So many times in the dark, the clothes looked like "monsters" to me. I shared one room with all of my sisters. There were six boys and four girls in my large family. I remember always waking my sister, Marilyn, up in the middle of the night to ask if I could sleep with her.

During the day I was very introverted and shy. After elementary school I felt that I was living in a cocoon. I always felt that I was fat and ugly; I didn't like my smile, so I stopped talking so much after my elementary years. It's amazing how the devil will hone in on the areas you are the most sensitive about. People would always make negative comments about my weight and that would ruin my day all the time.

The truth of the matter was that I wasn't fat at the time, but the devil was working to create a low self-esteem in me. I always thought that I weighed too much. I never liked the way I looked in my clothes—because I didn't like me. When I look back in retrospect, I realize that as *Psalm 139:14-15* says, **I will praise thee, for I am fearfully and wonderfully made: marvelous are thy works and that my soul knoweth right well. My substance was not hid from thee when I was made in secret and curiously wrought in the lowest part of the earth.** You see it is predestined before we are born how we will look and what kind of personality we will have. My prayer is that people will learn at an early age that "God does not make junk." The sooner we embrace this truth, the quicker we will be able to move and walk in the fullness of God.

I thank God for my parents because they were very supportive and caring. My dad went to work at Westinghouse every day, and my mom was an elementary school teacher. I can still remember the smell of my dad's lunch box and dipper that he used to take food in to his work everyday. It always made me hungry just to smell it. I never could figure out why anything my dad ate smelled so good and sounded so good as he crunched on it. I think this was symbolic of the spiritual food that our Heavenly Father has for us. As He speaks to us about His food, it whets our appetites and causes us to hunger and thirst after righteousness; **"Blessed are they who hunger and thirst after righteousness for they shall be filled."** *Matthew 5:6*

My mom was the type of person I could talk to about anything, except when she put her glasses on. To my child's mind, when she put on those glasses, that meant she had some business to take care of. So I was afraid to approach her. My mother always understood. She was wise, caring, but very firm. She didn't say, "I love you" a lot, but she demonstrated her love every day.

My dad, on the other hand, was stern and very fussy. He was a perfectionist and required the same of his children. We had a list of chores to do around the house, and he made sure they were done well. The interesting thing about my dad, though, was that he could *and would* do all of the things that he asked us to do.

When I say my dad was fussy, I mean he was fussy. He would talk about an issue that angered him for hours at a time. It may not have bothered my brothers so much, but I never enjoyed hearing two to three hours of lecturing (even though it was to someone else). My dad was a provider for our family. Every Friday when he got paid, he and my mom would sit down and work out the bills and what had to be paid. But back then, in our home, children couldn't ask a lot of questions, especially when grown-ups were talking. I remember seeing my dad stagger up the front steps (at least 15 or 16 of them) on the weekend. But I was a child and I didn't know that he had been drinking. I just remember that he looked differently and that I would sometimes be afraid that he would miss a step and fall. By the time I was old enough to understand the whole issue of drinking and alcoholism, my dad had been told by his doctor to stop, and he had stopped almost overnight. My dad was always such a disciplined person. I truly thank God for healing my dad at this point in my life because many of my brothers and sisters had experienced the effect of having an alcoholic father while God had protected me in this circumstance. God also caused my dad and me to grow together in His Word. We went to prayer meeting and Bible classes together for more than ten years before the Lord sent me to another church.

I remember the summer before my sophomore year in high school especially. It was a very traumatic time for me because I was in the band and we had to go away to band camp

7

somewhere between Vicksburg and Jackson at Percy Quinn State Park. I was a shy person and had not spent a great deal of time away from home. So I was very nervous. I had heard that the band director, Mr. Kermit Harness, was firm, and I was afraid I wouldn't make it in the band.

Mr. Harness actually turned out to be one of the best friends I ever had. He lived such a godly life before us that I came to regard him as a surrogate father in school. In my mind I can see Mr. Harness with a megaphone under his arm saying, "All right you guys, come close in the huddle—let's bow our heads for a word of prayer." He always talked to God as if he had a close personal relationship with Him. That always impressed me because it reinforced the power of prayer for me. We never did a show without praying. I feel sad when I think of schools today which don't allow band directors—or students—to pray before school events. If only we would go back to our foundation, "In God We Trust."

We had to get up early in the morning to go out to the field to learn how to march. As a matter of fact, it was before the sun came up every morning. Shortly after we had been there one morning, I remember standing in the dark field preparing to march when, all of a sudden, I realized something had happened to me. It felt like someone had turned the lights out inside me. I felt that I had died, but somehow was still alive. I felt like a separation had taken place inside me, and I didn't know what to do because I was in such a structured setting. My mom was a long way from me, so I didn't know what to do. So I just kept doing what everyone else was doing. This was a very traumatic time in my life because during this band camp, it felt as if God had walked away from me. I felt a separation take place on the inside of me. I felt like life had left me, but I was still alive in a mummy-like state. Even as I write this, I find it difficult and painful to explain the emotions I felt then. "How did this happen to me?" "What did I do wrong?" Those were the questions I asked myself. "Am I alive or dead?" It was as if I were able to see one moment, but became blind the next. It was as if I had died but was still alive. I was in a state of unreality. I really wasn't there anymore. So what do you do when you feel as if you are not alive, but you don't know how in the world to explain it? Well, what I did was—I kept moving along by the grace of God. It was one of the scariest moments of my life and it lasted for 20 years; yes, I said 20 years! It caught me by storm, but I didn't have any idea what to do about it. I felt like an alien from another planet. How do you tell your parents that you feel you've gone crazy? When I look back now I can remember the nights I prayed through the night that God would heal me. I told Him, "God, this is more than I can bear." But even as I write this book, and as the tears come back, I realize God was teaching me a lesson about His grace. Just as Paul begged God in *II Corinthians 12:8,* **For this thing I besought the Lord thrice, that it might depart from me;** so did I. For this thing I besought the Lord many times that it might depart from me. His answer to Paul was my answer for 20 years; *verse 9,* **And He said unto me, My grace is sufficient for thee: for my strength is made perfect in weakness. Most gladly therefore will I rather glory in my infirmities, that the power of Christ may rest upon me.**

My friend and co-worker Kay shared this scripture with me and it has now become my testimony. My healing from this depression didn't come until age 35, although it began when I was 15. The devil knew that I would preach the gospel with power and without compromise, thus tearing his kingdom down. So he tried to shut me up at an early age. "But God..."What God says will be, will be.

On February 3, 1995, when Jesus baptized me with the Holy Spirit, He also healed me. Hallelujah! Do I understand the grace of God? Yes, I do! You see, I'm not even supposed to be here to write this book, but God is delivering and healing some sisters and brothers now from depression and anxiety even as you read this book. Touch this page right now as a testament of your faith and believe God for your total healing. Hell's hounds are no match for our Mighty Lord and Saviour Jesus Christ!

When I got home from the camp I remember trying to tell my mom what had happened. But I had a hard time trying to explain. I remember sleeping a lot, and my family told me I acted strange and lost quite of bit of weight. I always wondered what was wrong with me. I thought I had a serious medical problem that was slowly killing me. But the interesting thing about my whole situation is that when I look back at all that I've gone through, I absolutely know that God has had His Hand on my life from the beginning of my existence. And even in the midst of all that was happening, I had good grades, was inducted into the Honor Society, was elected President of the Honor Society, was on the Student Council, and involved in so many things that people had no idea of the inner struggle I was going through.

I remember that I somehow got to go see the family doctor. And when he came in, he began to tell me how proud he was of me, and that he had seen my picture and name in one of the local newspapers all of the time. Then he asked me why I was there. I was too embarrassed to tell him all of the details, but I told him the critical ones. I told him about the sleeplessness, the nervous feelings, and about feeling strange and alien. The next question he asked me was, "Have you been hearing any voices talking to you?" I told him I had not, and at that point I was feeling uneasy about his question because it seemed to insinuate that I was either crazy or having some mental problems. The doctor was very open with me and told me at the end of our discussion that I was suffering from depression. I told him I wasn't upset about anything. But at this point in my life my knowledge about depression was very limited. He explained the disease to me and told me I could either take medicine to control it or wait to see if it would get any better on its own. I told him I wanted to think about it. So we scheduled another visit for me to come back and discuss my decision.

After praying and thinking the whole situation through, I decided that I wouldn't ever bring this subject up again because I didn't want anyone to talk to me or to see me as someone with a mental problem. My solution: I suppressed all of my feelings about myself. I told the doctor at the next appointment that I didn't want to take any medicine. He seemed happy about my decision. I also told him I was doing fine and felt much better, though that wasn't true. My decision basically was to just try to make it and to act normal even if I didn't <u>feel</u> normal.

There is no one who can ever tell me that prayer is not one of the most powerful tools God has given us. For the 20 years of my life that I struggled with this depression, God was always there.

I remember asking God when I was praying one night, "Who am I?" I asked Him if I were a human being or an angel because I was seemingly able to make it through all of the storms that came my way. I knew that I couldn't have been alive and able to do all that I was doing unless God was in total control. Not only was I "surviving"; I was also "thriving." People knew me and respected me greatly. I was called upon to do things and to speak at many churches even in college. I had mastered the art of hiding behind a mask and pretending I was doing fine. The difficult times came at night when reality would stare me in the face. I got married the last semester of my senior year at Millsaps College, but I still struggled with the depression.

In 1993, the church that I was a member of, Mt. Zion #1 Missionary Baptist Church, elected a new pastor, Reverend R.L. Forman. I could tell he was different from any other preacher I had ever known. He was open, honest, and filled with the Holy Ghost. I had previously had no accurate teaching on the Holy Ghost. But Pastor Forman believed in the laying on of hands and supernatural healing from God. He also believed in the biblical teaching that women were used by God to preach His Word. When I met him, he had two sisters who were already in the ministry, and he was very supportive of them. When he started having Bible study at the church during the day, I made sure I attended because I could tell he was a scholar in the scriptures. During the year that I studied with Pastor Forman I grew a lot and began to learn more about who the Holy Spirit was, His work, and His gifts. When God has a work for you to do, He always sends a John the Baptist before you to prepare the way: *Isaiah 40:3,* **The voice of him that crieth in the wilderness, Prepare ye the way of the LORD, make straight in the desert a highway for our God.** Jesus never sent His disciples out without proper preparation. In order for us to be effective in the ministry, we must submit to God's school of preparation. It varies from one individual to another, but the manual (The Bible) remains the same.

During this time and the year that followed, Pastor Forman began to tell me that there was an anointing on my life to preach. I had heard others say the same thing, but it never registered. In the meantime, my daughter, Ann, who was born May 22, 1992, had been having what her pediatrician called the "breath-holding syndrome." It manifested itself like seizures to me. She would cry in a certain way and then all of a sudden would throw her head back and just collapse. These seizure-like manifestations would totally stress me out when they happened. There were not many nights when I wouldn't have to get up and console my baby for hours at a time. To me it seemed that nothing appeased her for long. I would walk her, sing to her, talk to her, but nothing seemed to work. I was so stressed out with my new baby, as were her dad and brother. I spent many hours crying and praying for her. One of the things God showed me then was that He was going to use my child mightily, and the enemy was battling this. And as I was getting closer to the road of destiny that God had planned for me, the deceiver was trying to speed up His plan to send me over the edge mentally and physically. The sound of my baby's cry was so shrill that it pained us every time we heard her cry. She was on medication at first, but it didn't help. So I took her off. One night, after one of those episodes, I called my pastor and began to tell him about this, and how painful it was for me to see my baby like this. His response was, "Sister, this is nothing but a trick of the devil." He told me he was going to pray for her right then, but that he wanted my husband and me to bring her to church the next day so that he could anoint her with oil and lay hands on her. I felt more relieved after that phone call than I had been in a long time.

God is so faithful! The next day when Ann began to cry, I looked at her because the cry was totally different. It sounded more normal than I had heard it sound since she was a baby. I started crying myself because I knew that God had really healed my daughter. After all of the sleepless and restless nights of calming her down and being worried about the future, God had used Pastor Forman's phone prayer to do tremendous things for my daughter and for my faith. My husband and I did take Ann to the church and God did truly heal her. There were times when Ann still had the seizure-like episodes though, and my stress level would rise again—until I remembered what my pastor had taught me about how to keep a healing. Every time my daughter would have an episode after this, the devil would speak to me and say, "I told you she wasn't healed." I had to fight very hard through standing on the Word in order to battle this attack on her healing. On many occasions, too numerous to recount, God used Benny Hinn and Bishop T.D. Jakes' television ministries to pull me out of the pit of hell. There were many nights when I would be up in the middle of the night trying to figure out what to do when a Mighty Word from Heaven would come from these two men of God. How I thank God for the avenues He uses to keep us out of the claws of death and despair. I was also **Eating Along The Way!** to the healing ministry that God has day by day caused me to enter. I learned a lot through these additional situations about how to "keep" a healing that God does. I continued to believe that my daughter was healed, and I kept thanking God for what He had done. It was during this time that I learned about the tricks of the devil and how to fight them with the Word and with faith. It was also during this time that I learned that the scripture, "Death and life are in the power of the tongue," *Proverbs 18:21,* **"Death and life are in the power of the tongue: and they that love it shall eat the fruit thereof"** was real. I began

17

to be very conscious about what I spoke. Through this, the full manifestation of Ann's healing was seen.

Needless to say, my faith was growing by leaps and bounds. And I found that my confidence in my new pastor was growing. One night, I turned to him and told him that I wanted to tell him something, but didn't know if I could. He encouraged me to try, so I reached way down in the annals of my life and pulled out a painful box. I told him about how I had been struggling with myself on the inside and how I had felt that I was in a cocoon by myself for so long. I talked about my depression symptoms and how suppressed I felt on the inside. After I finished elaborating, my heart was thudding because I didn't know what his response would be. Would he also ask (as did the only other person I had confided in) if I had been hearing voices? Instead, my pastor laughed and said, "Sister, every minister that God has chosen has a testimony just like yours." He told me that when God calls us to a mighty work, the devil works hard to change our destiny and to totally discourage us. I felt so liberated after those words though I never acknowledged—or even felt then—that God was calling me into the ministry. I did not realize that I was **Eating Along The Way!** to my appointed destiny. God was feeding me spiritually all of the elements I would need when my season came. And it felt very good to confide something that had been bothering me for years to another human being who was sensitive to the Holy Spirit's leading.

On February 3, 1995, God used my neighbors, pastors Ollie and Enid Hardaway of Faith Christian Center to lay hands on me to pray for me to receive the baptism of the Holy Spirit. At this point in my life I was so very hungry and thirsty for more of God. I realized through my pastor and the relationship I had developed with Dr. Ollie Hardaway at work that there were more "rooms" in the Kingdom of God than what I had previously experienced. I literally felt God "calling" me to greater heights. I had been a teacher of many Bible Study Classes for more than twelve years and had spoken throughout the community for various programs. I thought that my gift of teaching was all that God had called me to do.

It was actually Co-Pastor Enid Hardaway who laid hands on me to receive the baptism in the Holy Spirit after a two-hour Bible study with the two of them. Dr. Hardaway went upstairs to pray as God was working some things out in me. I remember saying to Sister Hardaway, "I know that I'm saved and I know that the Holy Spirit is in me, but I do desire more of Him to be

19

in control." I told them both, since they had shown me in the scriptures that there was a lot more, that I wanted all that God had for us believers. I've never been a person to hesitate receiving anything from God when I know that it's Him. I did have the manifestation of the speaking in tongues that night, though it was only a few words. I remember saying only "conda la shonda:" and wondering if I were really filled and baptized in the Holy Ghost. This did not sound like speaking in tongues to me, but Dr. and Sister Hardaway did an excellent job helping me to understand that I would have to continue speaking in tongues daily in order for the "flow" to come. I thanked Sister Hardaway and Pastor Hardaway, but I left thinking to myself that I didn't know if that experience was real or not. I even questioned myself about whether or not speaking in tongues was real. But Sister Hardaway had given me a book to read that she said the Lord had laid on her heart to put in my hands, **Good Morning Holy Spirit**, by Benny Hinn.

When I got home I went into my bedroom. I was alone because at this time my husband was on the road, driving an 18-wheeler. I can remember very vividly lying in my bed looking up at the ceiling and feeling an overwhelming peace. I had never experienced a feeling like that in my life. As a matter of fact, I needed peace more than I needed anything else in my life. All of a sudden my room felt like it had been transformed from my room into heaven. I felt what had to be "glory" as I laid in my bed. It was at that moment that I realized that the baptism in the Holy Spirit was real. I felt God's presence in my room all night long. I found myself praising him in a way that I had never done before. I had always been a conservative worshipper and quite content with it at the time. On this night, though, I recognized the presence of God in my room and I became radical in thanking Him, and I thank God that I am still radical today in my praise! The Holy Spirit had brought me into an intimacy with my Father that I had never known; neither had I known that such a place of worship was possible. The next day I began reading the book, **Good Morning Holy Spirit**, and I could not put it down. I cried the whole time I was reading this book, but I didn't know why.

On Sunday, February 5, 1995, as I got to page 151, I was crying even more and all of a sudden the Holy Spirit spoke to me and said, *You have been filled, you have been praying to be healed for a long time, you are now healed, and you have been called to preach.* I couldn't believe what I heard as I read this book. I cried even more as he showed me the places in the book where I had had visions that I never understood but were similar to what Benny Hinn had described: the open-air stadiums, my standing in front of thousands of people talking, and so many other things. The Holy Spirit repeated again that I had received three things:

1) I had been filled with the Holy Spirit

2) I had now been healed of my depression

3) I was being called into the ministry to preach.

I was so shocked that I called my pastor even though it was midnight. His wife said she had already known it. The pastor said he wasn't surprised. He encouraged me and then we hung up. It was a while before it dawned on me that I had previously not believed that God used women to preach. It's interesting when God speaks, His voice is so distinct that you know that it's Him.

I had encouraged a female friend of mine about a month earlier who felt God was calling her into the ministry. I knew she was sincere and I knew her love for the Lord. So it was easy to tell Beveraly to go on and do what the Lord was telling her to do. Now, I had to eat my own words and accept the call. I asked

God to confirm this call into the ministry to me. He (The Holy Spirit) reminded me that the night before he spoke to me, he had Pastor Forman say to me very firmly that whether I acknowledged it or not, there was a call on my life to preach. I then had a powerful dream in which my calling was confirmed. In the dream, I was standing in the middle of a circle of many, many things that the Holy Spirit said would not yet be revealed. What was revealed was a pulpit in the center of the circle, which had about nine steps beside it. I then heard a voice that said, *"Preach the Word,"* about three times. The voice was very commanding and there was no doubt that this was the voice of God. The other things that were on the perimeter of the circle puzzled me, but I was sure one of them was my drama ministry. The implication was that whatever else it was that would be coming, it would all tie into the preaching of the gospel.

I must stop here to let you know that I have never been a person who put much stock in dreams; nor had I any confidence in people who talked about visions until God began to deal with me very personally through His Holy Spirit. I am very obviously a believer now! My prayer is that those of you who are reading my book now would believe even "before you have seen."

I remember asking my pastor, "Pastor, what did the steps mean that God showed me in my dream." His response was, "The steps represent levels in the ministry and in your walk with God." He said that God would advance me higher and higher as I remained faithful to Him and to His Holy Word. I have found all of this advice to be true as I move towards my seventh year in the ministry. My Lord has supplied my every need, and my greatest desire even now is to please Him in every way! He showed me a vision of the Lake of Fire and I audibly heard the sounds of weeping and gnashing of teeth. The Lord was saying to me that there were a certain number of people who were assigned to be saved through my ministry and that I would be responsible for those people if I didn't accept my call.

I went to a church where a woman in the ministry, Evangelist Ann Brown whom I had known for a long time, invited me to attend. Her pastor, Reverend Gibson, was flowing in the gifts of the spirit at the end of the service when, all of a sudden, I was singled out and asked to stand. This had never happened to me before. So I was very nervous, but I stood.

He spoke by the Spirit and said, "The Spirit of the Lord is upon you and He has called you to preach. The Lord said for you to go forth. He is healing you now." I remember that the date was March 26, 1995, because the Holy Spirit led me to begin a journal of prophecies and other important events. Pastor Gibson and I had never met. I knew that this was God because there was no way that Pastor Gibson would have known that this was the scripture that God had given me. God said through him, *"I'm sending you forth as a consuming fire. Listen to what I say to you. No one will be able to hurt you. I'll cause you to stand."* The Holy Spirit was demonstrating the powerful gift of prophecy to me even at an early stage in my ministry. I could do nothing but cry because this was another confirming word in addition to the dream and vision.

As I lay in my bed I remember saying (in such a childlike way), "Holy Spirit, I want to hear your voice." All of a sudden in my right ear I heard a distinct "voice" that said, *"You said you wanted to hear my voice; so here it is."* I was stunned beyond belief. The voice sounded almost like a child's voice, but it was distinctly commanding. By the way, my right ear has never been the same since that day. When God has me listening intently to a spiritual message, it's usually especially in my right ear that I "hear" supernatural revelation. There are even times now when my right ear acts as a sensor and begins to make a specific sound. This usually alerts me to the fact that

God is trying to tell me something when I may not be tuned into things as I should. It's almost like an on/off switch.

This same night I asked the Holy Ghost to tell me what my gift was. When I think about it now, that was not an appropriate question because there may be many gifts of the Holy Spirit that may manifest strongly in a believer's life after they are filled with the Holy Ghost. And just like God, He dealt with me according to my knowledge. He answered my question by putting the word on my wall in front of me as though it were a screen. The word "PROPHECY" appeared in red and bold print. I absolutely knew that the Holy Spirit was real by now. I had no clue about what the word "prophecy" meant in this context. I had heard the word before in Sunday School and in a couple of other places, but I had no idea what the spirit of God was saying to me on this night. I later called Co-Pastor Enid Hardaway and she explained it in fuller detail. I've seen this gift manifest more and more as I have gone forward in the ministry. I discover more and more that prophecy happens when you divorce yourself from your own mind and flesh and allow the Holy Spirit to have total reign over the words that you speak. When this is done, He speaks directly to the people who are present at that time in that setting, a specific word of exhortation, encouragement, and/or consolation. The word is so "specific" that those who are listening absolutely know that "God" is speaking through you because the Holy Spirit is revealing their inner thoughts.

When I first got filled with the Holy Ghost I remember being in my prayer closet (my bathroom) a lot. I spent hours praying and seeking God's face because the Holy Spirit had brought me to a new level of intimacy with my Father. On one of those occasions of prayer, I looked up and could not believe my eyes. I saw creatures flying in the air right before my eyes. They looked like eagles, and there were a lot of them. In my mind I kept thinking that I should be shocked, but in the Spirit I knew that I was in another dimension and was keenly aware of the presence of God.

I did say, "Holy Spirit, what are these?"

His response was, *"Ministering spirits."* I didn't understand it altogether, but I asked no more questions. That was about six years ago and I still see the ministering spirits around me on a daily basis. Many times they move up and down as though they are on a ladder. When I first began to see them I could see them very clearly. Now, I see them, but they are only very distinct when the Spirit of God is saying some things to me that I really need to get in tune with. I am always awake and alert when I see them. The Holy Spirit uses them strongly to get my attention. The scriptural basis for this that was given to me by God is *Hebrews 1:14*: **Are they not all ministering spirits, sent forth to minister for them who shall be heirs of salvation?**

God really prepared me for my ministry even when I didn't see what He was doing. When I was in high school, I was very active in church and was a Sunday School teacher. I had formerly held the offices of Church Reporter, Sunday School Secretary, and for 17 years, Assistant Secretary of the church. I was called by God all the way from the back of the church to the pulpit. What a hard time I had making this adjustment. When I was in high school, I remember talking to my friends a lot about the Sunday School lessons each week, and I always did a weekly quiz on "what the lesson was about." I could look at the expressions on their faces that showed, "Please don't ask me any questions today." I would be on fire about everything that I was learning. As far back as I can remember, I have always loved the Word. In college I was still motivated to study the Word because I had met several girls who were upperclassmen and they were having weekly Bible Study groups. Many of them were members of Alpha Kappa Alpha Sorority, Inc. and would talk to me about joining. I did join in the fall of '81, and this led to an even closer bond in our studying the Word of God.

I had a "Soror" (my sister from the sorority) whom God used mightily to impress some things on me. Her name was Linda, too. She was tall, petite, and had a wonderfully kind smile. Linda loved to laugh and to joke, but she was very focused on staying "straight" for the Lord and was focused on her education. Linda was also a very smart young lady. I was very impressed by the fact that she was still a virgin and was in her sophomore year at Millsaps College.

During my years at Millsaps, there were not many black students who lived on campus or even attended there. Many of the black students on campus therefore were very closely knit. We had a lot of Bible Studies in Linda's room because she was the teacher and because she was the most committed and consistent one when it came to staying on our weekly schedule.

One discussion I remember that my roommate, Bonnie Rogers, and I brought up in particular was whether or not God cared if we went out to nightclubs or to a party as long as we were "true Christians." Linda did a lot of research, and we all

29

began to search the scriptures more to hear from God about this topic. The final answer was a little sad news for us because our sorority believed in "cube" parties in our dormitories. But the answer from the Word was, **"Wherefore come out from among them, and be ye separate, saith the Lord, and touch not the unclean thing; and I will receive you,"** *II Corinthians 6:17.* I remember still trying to change the Lord's mind about this issue in my personal prayer time. But I never succeeded! One of my good friends on campus was Beveraly, and many times during Bible Class she would get "happy" (emotionally zealous) and cry or shout. She really loved the Lord, even back then, and was not ashamed to show it. There were a lot of people on campus who didn't understand this "Christian Group" because most of them were very "academically" oriented. There was an older man who used to come to some of our Bible Classes back then. God really used him to spur me on to study and to memorize scriptures. I don't think we ever developed a friendship at all. I got opportunities to hear him minister the Word, and I was always impressed with the fact that he knew where the scriptures came from. I remember thinking that I wanted to know where scriptures were when I was talking to others about God. God used this thought to motivate me in my studies even before I began to preach.

After I graduated from college, God put me on a path of continuous study. I had gotten married in my last semester in college, so Tony and I had no children yet. I had a lot of time on my hands and lot of desire in my heart to know the Lord according to His Word. I had begun to attend a local community-wide Bible Class because we had not established one at the church I was attending. The class was good, but it was not really meeting my needs. I felt we were going through too many chapters too quickly each week. I was not digesting the meat of what was going on in the passages. I did continue to attend until I met a bald-headed, soft-spoken, older gentleman whom God used to totally change my life. He came in to teach for a few weeks because our teacher had to go out of town. His name was Ben Peterson, Sr., and we all called him "Bro' Pete."

The first time I heard him teach came the famous words he would use after expounding on scripture; "You get the idea?" he would ask. I had no idea that I would be hearing those words for more than a decade to come. Needless to say, I fell in love with his teaching style and his bubbly personality. When his time was up for teaching, I asked him where his class was, and found myself moving to another Bible Class shortly thereafter.

The church where Bro' Pete taught was way out in the country. As a matter of fact, I got lost trying to find it the first time. The church was an old white wood building; very traditional-looking with nothing about it that stood out. But when you went into the building, there was so much love there. Bro' Pete always sat in the front on the right hand side (normally the Mothers' Board side), and he usually dressed in an old style suit and hat, and he always had a joke to tell. He loved to laugh and he was extremely intelligent. Bro' Pete had to have been in his late 70s when I met him, but was the type to attract people of all ages. We all loved him.

Bro' Pete was an excellent teacher. His style of teaching was just what I had been looking for. Many times our hour and a half Bible Class consisted of teaching from one scripture. He knew how to dissect a scripture to get all of the meat from it. When he finished teaching, most of us knew where that scripture was found and we knew it by memory.

One of his favorite scriptural sayings was, "Have you heard? Have you seen?" *II Timothy 3:16:* **All scripture is given by inspiration of God, and is profitable for doctrine, for**

reproof, for correction, for instruction in righteousness. And his question would be, "What does it say?" We were quizzed each Wednesday night in this Bible Class. He did what he termed "blackboard demonstrations."

These were scriptural lessons on posters that had powerful bullet points. He kept them rolled up in the back of the church and pulled them out as he was led to use them. God was teaching me a lot during these years about His Word and how to diligently seek Him for revelation knowledge. As the years went by, I had discovered that I had a disdain for preachers, didn't believe that God called women into the ministry, and that salvation was based on works. God later gave me a revelation in these areas that pulled me out of these Bible Classes. I had learned the things He wanted me to learn and now He was moving me on. When I look back I thank God for Bro' Pete and his amazing teaching because he taught me the things that he understood and knew and believed. God now was calling me to a higher revelation of Himself and His Kingdom. This was a very difficult adjustment for me because I was very bonded to the people that I had been studying the Word with for so long. I've found, though, that on this journey with God, we have to be open to changes and deeper revelations. *Ephesians 1:18:*

"The eyes of your understanding being enlightened; that ye may know what is the hope of his calling, and what the riches of the glory of his inheritance in the saints." There is fullness in Him and we can only achieve it as we walk daily with Him and deny ourselves. *Luke 9:23*, **And He said to them all, If any man will come after me, let him deny himself, and take up his cross daily, and follow me** and allow the spirit of God to be the chief leader.

At the same time that I was attending this Wednesday Bible Class I was faithfully attending a Friday night Bible Class for just as long. The teacher of this class was a tall, slender, light-complexioned, but handsome elderly pastor of a local church. He had been an evangelist and crusader most of his life. God had recently called him to pastor. His name was Reverend Harold Green. He was the teacher and was very articulate and knowledgeable. Bro' Pete also attended this class. There was friction between these two gentlemen at times because Reverend Green, whom we called "Bro' Green" at that time believed that God did call women into the ministry, and that salvation was by grace and not by works.

I was for many years torn between these two teachers' doctrines. Reverend Green and I were also very close and he told me numerous times, before he died of a massive heart attack, that he had been listening to my comments in the class and could hear that God was using me in a mighty way. He said that I was getting the kind of revelation that God was giving him. Reverend Green also told me that God had shown him that there would be some women preachers coming forth from this Friday Class. I laughed every time he said this to me because he intimated very directly that I was one of them. I didn't believe it and I told him that. I did, however, come to the revelation that salvation is by grace alone. God taught me this lesson by His spirit and told me to "never forget it." When Reverend Green's church celebrated its 100th anniversary, he asked me to be the speaker. He insisted that I speak from the pulpit. When I look back over this I see how God gave him a glimpse of my preaching ministry even before he died. He was so excited about whatever God gave me to say on that day. If I could have a conversation with him today, I would want to apologize for not embracing the great truths he taught me. I thank God so much even now for things he said and did during my preparation stage for the ministry. Reverend Green knew who I was before I did. *Romans 11:33,* **O the depth of the riches both of the wisdom and knowledge of God! how**

unsearchable are His judgments, and His ways past finding out! God's ways *are* past finding out.

CHAPTER TWO

THE BATTLE

Now my life had changed overnight. When I told my husband about the call into the ministry, the conversation was not quite as I had imagined that it would be. He was on the road driving, so the conversation was by telephone. "Tony," I remember saying, "God has called me into the preaching ministry and I can't deny it because I have never experienced what I have recently experienced." I then went on to tell him about all of the things God had done and spoken to me.

His response was, "Linda, I think this decision is about Beveraly. Since God has called her into the ministry, I think you probably think God has called you too. I also told you about hanging around the pastor and the assistant pastor so much. I think this is why you feel God has called you into the ministry."

I was devastated but I had told him at the beginning of the conversation that I would not go forward without him being beside me and in agreement with the assignment I had received from my Father. After we hung up, I cried and told the Lord that if this was truly Him, I knew He would work it out. I had also told my husband that I would not tell anyone else about the call.

Before this day was over, my husband had stopped to call me back. He apologized and told me, "Do what the Lord has instructed you to do. Don't wait; go ahead and tell the church publicly—even though I won't be there physically, I'll be there spiritually." Needless to say, I cried some more, but this time they were tears of joy because I knew this had been a miracle occurrence. My husband was not quick to apologize, nor to make a decision, nor change his mind so quickly. God was truly at work. He said he would support me in the ministry, and he has done that even to this very hour.

I must admit that I was terrified concerning what the future held for me as a woman in the ministry. I knew of no women in the Baptist faith who had been supported by their church or pastor once they announced their call into the ministry. The devil fought me so hard mentally that I remember shortly after coming forth that I went to the pastor and told him I wanted to tell the church that I had *not* been called to preach. Everything started happening negatively to me and with me. My thinking seemed to be eroding. I couldn't concentrate much on anything. I started having one problem after another. I kept thinking surely all of this wouldn't be happening if I were truly called to the ministry. My pastor assured me (though he laughed at first) that all of this was spiritual warfare and that it ***actually*** meant that God had called me, but the enemy didn't want to see me go forth. Dr. Hardaway also explained to me that the more you go through, the greater the call of God is on your life. All of this helped a lot, but I discovered that the Holy Spirit was my ultimate teacher and that there were things that I would have to experience in order for me to do what I had been ordained to do.

I was disappointed by a lot of people who, I thought, would pray for and encourage me. I had a friend (a woman) whom I had known for a long time and that I gave my testimony (excitedly) to concerning my call into the ministry. When I finished, she didn't even look me in the eyes. She just said, "Oh."

That hurt me a lot, but it caused me to grow up a lot. The people I thought would be supportive were not that way at all. The ones whose excitement and enthusiasm I least expected were the ones who came up to me and said that they already knew that I would one day preach the gospel. A lot of the members in my church at Mt. Zion were loving, kind, and prayerful. But one of the deacons pulled me to the side one day and told me he had received a phone call from someone in the church after I had made my announcement. He never gave me the name, but said he couldn't believe that God had called me. I had a lot of patience with people who felt like this because I never believed myself (didn't know the Word) that God would use a woman to carry the gospel. Needless to say, there were women as well as men who tried to discourage me from going forth.

Pastor Forman taught me pulpit etiquette and showed me the ropes in the ministry. Unlike some other pastors, he was the same with me when he was in a group with other preachers and pastors as he was when we were in our home church. He stressed the importance of allowing people to call me by my ministry title as well as sitting in the pulpit whenever it was allowed in other churches. This was good teaching for me because at this point in my life, what people called me or where I sat was not important to me. I also learned the importance of submission to the godly leadership the Lord had placed over my life.

I went through some very uncomfortable seasons. I knew to always contact the pastor of a church whenever I was invited to minister at a service. There were times when I would feel very nervous about going into a church because I never knew what the response would be from the pastors. I was invited to minister at a church in Meridian. When I got there, I told the usher who I was and she immediately told me that the pastor of this church was on vacation and he did not allow women in the pulpit. There were some other men in the pulpit. But sitting in the pulpit was not the issue for me. The issue was why you would invite a woman to your church who had publicly spoken of her call to the ministry when you have an issue with this.

In some other churches, women in the ministry were asked to sit on the Mothers' Board. The pastors would address me as "Evangelist" Linda Sweezer, but did not allow me to sit where the "men" in the ministry sat. So what did I do? I kept praying and I kept going because I knew beyond the shadow of a doubt that God had called me into the ministry.

One of the things the Holy Spirit said to me early in my ministry was **not** to fight men who fought my ministry. He told me to *"preach the Word"* and that He would open doors for me. He also told me not to seek to be justified by others. This was important that the Holy Spirit ministered to me because I did want to hear people say (at the beginning of my ministry) that they believed that God had called me to preach. As I moved further in my ministry, the Holy Spirit always encouraged me along the way with spiritual food that many couldn't see. Every time I sat down after a sermon and felt discouraged, the Spirit of God would whisper (and still does), "You spoke what I told you to speak and I'm pleased." He would also send people or have someone to call me with a word of encouragement afterwards. I also learned quickly that the devil not only uses the issue of, "Is a woman called to preach?" as a way to divide and conquer, but uses many other issues as well such as:

1) Should women wear pants?
2) Should there be music in the worship service?
3) Are you saved if you are baptized in the name of the Father, Son, and the Holy Ghost only?
4) Are you saved if you do not speak with other tongues?
5) Was Jesus really God?
6) Is the devil real?

7) When we die, do our souls go immediately into the presence of the Lord?

8) Is Christianity a white man's religion?

9) Does God really want us to prosper financially?

10) Is hell a real place?

The list goes on and on. Since the devil uses the "same old soup just warmed over," the debate about women in the ministry did not surprise me. That fact alone has put to rest many of my issues with people who struggle when a woman is called to preach.

The devil's goal in any situation or circumstance is to divide. God's goal is always to unify through the blood of Jesus Christ.

One of the great blessings I have received from the Lord is being able to be rejected but still walk in love towards my brothers in the ministry. One of the valuable lessons that I have learned is that because God has called and chosen you, there are people and audiences waiting on the word God has given exclusively to you. Every time Paul was rejected in a city there were people waiting to hear the Word through him in another city. I have been very encouraged by the people whom I have met who were "hungering" and "thirsting" after righteousness. Their desire to hear the Word and to walk in the Word has encouraged me to persevere in the things of God, to pray more fervently, and "to study to show myself approved unto God." *II Timothy 2:15,* **Study to shew thyself approved unto God, a workman that needeth not be ashamed, rightly dividing the word of truth.** I am motivated to keep going every time I get a phone call, every time I hear a knock at the door, every time I'm stopped in the store or the mall and I hear people say, "you really helped me because I was getting ready to kill myself, I was getting ready to kill someone else, I was thinking about leaving the church for good. I've been so depressed that I started taking anti-depressants but I don't need them now, God really does love me, God really has been hearing my prayers, I've stopped drinking, I've stopped using drugs, I've decided to take a stand for Jesus even at school, I've got my joy back."

These are the words of motivation that make me say, I've got to keep going. You see, I understand that God has not called me into the ministry to join the ministerial social club. If that were the case, then I could at least have formed a support group of women in the ministry. God has not called me or you to be a part of the clique, but He has called us "alone" to make a difference with the "multitude."

As I reflect back over the years, I see how God used me first as a teacher of His Word. After years of being in Bible Study classes two to three times a week and sometimes being the only woman present, I see how God was preparing my life for this hour. I had such a hunger for God's Word that even in college we had weekly Bible Studies in each other's rooms. I had a desire (that God put there) to know Him better.

I was surprised to find a love letter that I had written in high school to my boyfriend, now my husband. In the letter there were references even then to my faith and confidence in God. I didn't even remember being that serious about my walk with God even while I was in high school until I found that love letter. I then began to reflect on the fact that I was teaching Sunday School while I was in high school. The call of God was heavy on my life even when I didn't recognize it. In church I sang in the Junior Choir, was secretary and assistant secretary of the Sunday School, was the announcer for the church, Sunday School teacher, Bible Class teacher, and was the assistant secretary of the church for 17 years before God spoke and said for me to come from the back of the church to the pulpit. He is an awesome God! He has been teaching and feeding me from the table of humility all of my life. That's why this vessel is a broken vessel with no agendas except for those that come from Heaven.

As I continued to walk with God He led me to write plays. I had always written skits in church for the children to perform. In 1992, my first major play was written and performed at the local theater. It was entitled, "One in Christ." From here the Lord began to exalt me before the community. My name was always in the newspaper and on the Jackson radio and television stations. The scripture says in *I Peter 5:6,* **Humble yourselves therefore under the mighty hand of God, that he may exalt you in due time.** God exalts us only for His glory and honor, not for our own.

There was a man who stopped me one day and asked me if I had plans to run for any political office. I asked him why he was asking me this question and he said it was because I was always in the paper and on the radio. I explained to him that I had no political ambitions but that the Holy Ghost was my "private agent" for the Kingdom of Heaven's sake. It was obvious to me that this was not the expected response. What God is doing in my life is above anything I could even fathom.

Shortly after my call to the ministry the Holy Spirit led me into an incredible experience. It began with a prophetic word from a woman in the ministry at one of the local churches. I attended an evening service to support my sister in the ministry one Sunday night. I had just recently been filled with the Holy Ghost and was so excited although there were so many things about Him that I still didn't understand. During the Bible Class I had an incredible urge to speak in tongues. I knew I shouldn't do it because the evangelist was teaching and I would have been out of order. I was very quiet the entire night (very unusual for me) because I remember wondering if somehow "speaking in tongues" could come apart from my desire to do it. I was also wondering why I felt so out of control. I didn't understand at that time that **"And at the beginning of the scripture the spirits of the prophets are subject to the prophets. For God is not the author of confusion, but of peace, as in all churches of the saints."** *I Corinthians 14:32-33.* The Holy Spirit is a gentleman and He is very intelligent. He only leads us to do things that are decent and in order. I stayed even after the class was over because one of my friends was going to receive prayer that she might be filled with the Holy Ghost. I was very excited for her and wanted to stay around to see her joy and excitement afterwards. It took a long time because she was taken into the pastor's study along with the evangelist who had spoken previously that night. I greatly desired to be in the room when she was filled with the Holy Ghost, but was not allowed to come in until the end. When they did call me into the pastor's study, little did I know that I would be prayed for. My friend was all smiles as she told me that it had been a wonderful experience. The two ministers then began to pray for me. Evangelist Brown told me, "Take your shoes off because I've got to anoint them for the journey you are about to take." I had no idea what the Lord was saying to me through her.

She prayed for strength and protection for me. The pastor was in a corner of the room talking prophetically to me as the evangelist laid hands on me and anointed my feet with oil. He said, "The Lord says, open your eyes and see." There was also laughter that came from this pastor which was not from him, but from God. He was laughing under the anointing, and what I heard God say through this was that everything was all right and that He (God) was in control. At this point I was on the floor and the pastor said, "Go ahead and speak in tongues now." I then began to speak in tongues as I never had before, and I wasn't afraid. When I left out I felt an incredible weight off my shoulders. God had done great deliverance in and for me, but at this point I didn't fully understand what was happening. I did know, however, that the presence of the Lord was in the room. I really felt differently when I left that night. I somehow felt more alive. The Holy Spirit had me in a process. He was purging me and it felt good.

Not long after this prophetic event, I was scheduled to fly to Chicago for a three-day conference. I was on the steering committee for a caucus of a national coalition. I thought this would be a typical trip because our committee had met before. I knew the hotel where I was supposed to have reservations. So I took a cab there. But things were not so typical after all because, when I arrived at the hotel, they did not have any reservations for me and I did not have the number of the chairman of our committee. The lady at the reservation desk told me, though, that there was another hotel with a similar name not very far from this one and said that their shuttle van could take me there. I felt very relieved at this point because I didn't know what I was going to do. The van took me to an area of Chicago where I had not been before, and the driver pointed out a building that was to my right and said, "There it is." I thanked him, got off the van with all of my luggage, and walked up to the door of that building only to discover that it was not a hotel at all. The shuttle van had pulled off and there I was stranded in a remote area of Chicago, alone, carrying a lot of luggage, and, at this point, very afraid of who I might run into. It seemed to me that the obvious thing was to keep walking and see if I could locate this missing hotel. I was angry with myself for not bringing any contact phone numbers. Needless to say, I found no hotel in the area. At this point it started to rain and I was walking and walking, but to no avail. I was so frustrated that I began to cry and to pray. I remember looking up to the sky and saying, "God, what's going on?" As I walked, I noticed an elderly white man who was walking behind me. He was somewhat bent over and seemed to be struggling just to put one foot in front of the other one. He followed me for a long distance as I walked. At first I was afraid that he was going to try and mug me. I knew he appeared elderly and walked bent over, but there was something youthful about him in his face. After a while I felt relieved that he was back there. "At least," I thought, "there is someone around in this remote area". Every time I looked back at this man, he dropped his head and wouldn't look at me. At one point, I tried to ask him a question concerning my direction, but he didn't respond. He just dropped his head. It wasn't until this man literally disappeared before my eyes in front of a building we came to that I realized he wasn't from here. He had to have been an angel in disguise. This experience was so incredible that I didn't tell anyone about it for a long time. I had then only told one or two people I knew that this angel who was watching out for me was God's "provision" for a scared woman of God who was **Eating Along The Way!** God had an agenda for me. I did make it to a bus stop and I went back to the hotel I had been to originally. They now had reservations for me. The next day when I went down to the meeting rooms for the committee meeting, I could not find anyone. I just couldn't believe that this was happening to me. I did find a phone number of one of the members, but did not get an answer. I went back to my room again.

I had no idea that God did truly have me on a journey that I would never forget. I had relatives in the city, but I wasn't led to call any of them. Since I couldn't find the people I was supposed to meet with, I stayed in my room until late that evening. I remembered then that I had made some "prophetic" notes at a funeral not long ago. There were some people from

Chicago who spoke. They said the name of their church and I was led to write it down. Now that I was in Chicago the Spirit of God led me to this church and they were having Bible Class. I sat silently in the class and listened as Deacon Welch (an elderly gentleman who reminded me of Bro' Pete) taught expertly from the book of Psalms. The Spirit of God had given me a woman's name to ask for when I got there. At the end of the class during the announcement period this lady's name was read off the sick list. I almost jumped out of my seat when I actually heard the name called that the Holy Spirit had given me.

Afterwards, I asked some of the members who stayed late if they could tell me how to find the hospital where she was. I found out later she was actually in a nursing home. When I asked for directions, the teacher, Deacon Welch, insisted on taking me himself. I had never met or seen him before but I had the peace of God to go with him. He had a hard time finding this place and we were lost for about an hour and a half. During this time, we talked and I told him how I had no idea why I was at their church or why I was looking for this lady. I told him I felt God wanted me to pray for her. That was good enough for him. He obviously felt called to take me on this "mission for the

Lord." In the meantime, he told me, "I'm not the regular teacher of this class. I'm just filling in right now for the regular teacher who is ill." He was very open and easy to talk to. I told him my testimony about being filled with the Holy Ghost and being called to "preach." I thought that he would be a traditional-thinking person who would struggle with the issue of a woman preacher. He told me very directly that he knew God used women. He quoted many scriptures including *Joel 2:28*, **And it shall come to pass afterward, that I will pour out my spirit upon all flesh; and your sons and your daughters shall prophesy, your old men shall dream dreams, your young men shall see visions.** He said his struggle was with "speaking with other tongues." I got excited because I knew this was why we were together. I shared about all God had taught me up to this point about the baptism of the Holy Ghost. I sensed he was really listening, especially since I had come from a great distance. We were instant friends from that point. When we got to the nursing home, the security officer told us that they were closed. Deacon Welch charmed him into allowing us up for prayer anyway. When we got to the room I started to shake and tremble when I saw this lady because she looked like a witch. She was one of the most frightening women I had ever seen, but

I knew that I still had to pray for her. After Deacon Welch introduced us I walked over to her, laid my hands on her, and began to pray for her and for me. The Spirit of God was teaching me "boldness" and "faith" all at the same time. *Hebrews 11:6,* **But without faith it is impossible to please him: for he that cometh to God must believe that he is, and that he is a rewarder of them that diligently seek him.** I can't tell you how happy I was to leave out of that room! God's mission was accomplished and I was still alive! God was also teaching me that I would be battling with "principalities, powers, and rulers of the darkness of this world," and He wanted me never to be afraid. *Ephesians 6:12,* **For we wrestle not against flesh and blood, but against principalities, against powers, against the rulers of the darkness of this world, against spiritual wickedness in high places.** Deacon Welch took me back to my hotel and I knew from that night forward that I would never forget His "labor of love."

The next days were filled with crying and lamentation. I discovered that this journey was a "healing" journey. The Holy Ghost revealed to me during this sad time that I had suppressed a lot of my emotions from 1991 when my sister died. It was now 1995 and I still was not in touch with the fact that I felt that I had not done enough to save my sister's life. I had suppressed my "guilty" feelings because I knew how much my sister had always depended on me to be there for her. She had lost her nine-month child and was trying to deliver it when she arrested—right before my eyes. It was the most painful event that I had ever experienced because I felt so helpless. She and I were the youngest in a family of ten children. She was number nine and I am number ten. She would always call me "Puddin" and would tell people "She's my baby sister and I'm her baby sister." My sister, Flora, was the "life" of the family. She loved her parents and her family deeply. She was a "hugger" and a "big spender." She loved to give and was loved by so many. She always brought me Christian literature, and when I was promoted to Co-Director on my job in 1989, she brought me a briefcase and all kinds of office stuff that she thought I needed.

God healed a lot of suppressed pain and emotions during these three days. One of those nights I remember lying in bed and remembering the times I would get on my knees to pray, but would feel like I wanted to cry. I never would cry during those years because I wanted to be "strong" and I didn't understand that to God being strong means being "weak" in His presence. *II Corinthians 12:9*, **And he said unto me, my grace**

is sufficient for thee: For My strength is made perfect in weakness. Most gladly therefore will I rather glory in my infirmities, that the power of Christ may rest upon me. The Holy Spirit "fed" me with my own tears and enabled me to release it to Him. It is amazing that we can't even "cry" without the Holy Spirit's leading. Tears are God's way of cleansing us. The Lord was doing a great catharsis in my life through the work of the Holy Spirit. He was constantly leading me down the ministry road.

During this time of consecration and quiet time, the Lord began to give me His thoughts about abortion. This was critical because in order to share the gospel, you must know God's "heart" about many matters.

Abortion, to God, is murder, and we must understand it this way. God does forgive, and we must always balance the truth with His mercy and forgiveness. But for those of you who may be reading this book, it's critical that you repent if you have ever had an abortion or "supported" someone who did. We must teach our children abstinence as God's perfect will until such time that they decide to marry. God honors marriage. *Hebrews 13:4,* **Marriage is honorable in all, and the bed undefiled: but whoremongers and adulterers God will**

judge. If you have already repented, don't forget to tell someone else that God hates abortion. Our society talks about abortion as another method of birth control and we must go back to those who have embraced this false message and say, "God hates abortion."

The night before I left Chicago, as I was lying in bed, the Spirit of God told me to get up quickly because He had something he wanted to show me. I moved quickly under His leading to the elevator. Of course I didn't know which button to push. The elevator door closed quickly. A floor button was depressed (actually I saw many buttons light up). I went up to a floor very high up. The Holy Ghost then said *"to get off here"* (after the door opened on its own). There in front of me were a lot of people. There was music playing and people were very dressed up. All of a sudden I realized that this was a wedding. The Holy Spirit had already told me, *"You are going to get married."* I got to this event in time to see the bride go up the stairs. The groom met her and then the doors closed. I never saw the bride's face. Again I didn't understand what the Lord was saying then, but I now understand that I was the bride. God was taking me (and still is) to another level (ministry) and the intimacy was about to get greater. How I thank Him even today for showing me a "physical" manifestation of the "spiritual" reality that was going on in my own life, and what a supernatural way he used to get me to the scene. *Zechariah 4:5-6,* **Then the angel that talked with me answered and said unto me, Knowest thou not what these be? And I said, No my Lord. Then he answered and spake unto me, saying, This is the word of the LORD unto Zerubbabel, saying, Not by might, nor by power, but by my spirit, saith the LORD of hosts.** God is a supernatural God and He still uses supernatural means of getting His called ones to their destinations. That's what this entire "journey" was to Chicago. It was my "Arabian" teaching ground, *Galatians 1:15-17,* **But when it pleased God, who separated me from my mother's womb, and called me by his grace, To reveal His son in me, that I might preach him among the heathen; immediately I conferred not with flesh and blood: Neither went I up to Jerusalem to them which were apostles before me; but I went into Arabia, and returned again unto Damascus.**

During the wedding, there was a middle-aged white woman who stood by me. She was friendly and talkative. We talked about how beautiful the wedding had been. Afterwards, she asked me if she could see my room because she had never stayed in this hotel before. I took her to my room very innocently. She looked it over and then she asked me if I wanted to go down the street to see her hotel room. Well, at this point I started feeling nervous because I realized that I was not in small town Vicksburg, Mississippi, but in the big, rambunctious city of Chicago, Illinois. I also began to sense that she was probably a lesbian looking for another victim. I politely but firmly said no and walked her to the door. She had told me earlier that she was a nurse. I wanted to let her know at this point of understanding that I was not sick or in need of her "medicine." This experience, overall, taught me some valuable lessons:

1) God is the *source* of our strength. *Isaiah 40:31,* **But they that wait upon the LORD shall renew their strength; they shall mount up with wings as eagles; they shall run, and not be weary; and they shall walk, and not faint.**

2) When God has a call on your life, He will bring you to a point where there's no one but you and Him. *Matthew 11:28-29,* **Come unto me, all ye that labour and are heavy laden, and I will give you rest. Take my yoke**

upon you, and learn of me; for I am meek and lowly in heart: and ye shall find rest unto your souls.

3) God wants us totally dependent on Him and on His strength. *Ephesians 6:10*, **Finally, my brethren, be strong in the Lord, and in the power of his might.**

4) In order for God to use you, you must be "bold" enough to do His will without question or thought. *Isaiah 1:19*, **If ye be willing and obedient, ye shall eat the good of the land**; *1 Peter 1:14*, **As obedient children, not fashioning yourselves according to the former lusts in your ignorance.**

5) God will supply and meet all of our needs. *Philippians 4:19*, **But my God shall supply all your need according to his riches in glory by Christ Jesus.**

6) When you are in the will of God, He will protect you. *Psalms 27:5*, **For in the time of trouble he shall hide me in his pavilion: in the secret of his tabernacle shall he hide me; he shall set me up upon a rock.**

7) God takes us on many "journeys," but He always has a "plan." *Romans 8:28*, **And we know that all things work together for good to them that love God, to them who are the called according to his purpose.**

8) When God chooses you—seek His face and His will and His heart about matters, *Psalms 27:8,* **When thou saidst, Seek ye my face; my heart said unto thee, Thy face, LORD, will I seek.**

CHAPTER THREE

WALKING IN THE FULLNESS

Through many of the battles I have endured, God used my pastor to keep me encouraged, to affirm me during times of serious doubt and confusion, and to teach me proper pulpit etiquette. The week before I was to actually go into the pulpit was a time that I was very anxious and nervous. Some of the members of the church and I were in the fellowship hall with the pastor when I asked Pastor Forman to come to the front. "I know this sounds like a dumb request," I said to him, "but could you walk into the pulpit with me and let me get comfortable sitting up there?" He laughed and said he understood my nervousness. He said, "You don't have to be nervous, just trust God." I sat in the chair to the right of his in this 200-seat church where I had grown up. He then left me in the pulpit and sat in the pews. He told me to understand that I was a "woman of God who had been called" and that I had nothing to fear. Pastor Forman told me that usually people who are really nervous are those whose lives are not patterned according to the Word. He said that "as long as I was in the will of God I should have nothing to fear or to be afraid of." He then told me to sit in his chair. For me that was very difficult. All of a sudden the light above me flickered.

During my moments and times of confusion it seemed to me that my pastor always had a Word from heaven for me that fit just right. The Holy Ghost always gave him the right scripture. The blessing for me was that he never made me feel "foolish" or "stupid" during my early months and years of ministry. One day I remember that it seemed everything was going wrong. The devil was speaking all kinds of crazy things in my head to convince me that I wasn't called. I felt like I was losing my mind. My peace was gone and I didn't know who to turn to. God sent me to the church. I remember on this particular day that the pastor was sitting on the second seat or the Mothers' Board side. I sat on the first seat almost in tears seeking God with all of my heart. The pastor told me to turn *to Psalm 23,* **The Lord is my shepherd I shall not want. He maketh me to lie down in green pastures: he leadeth me beside the still waters. He restoreth my soul: He leadeth me in the paths of righteousness for his name's sake. Yea, though I walk through the valley of the shadow of death, I will fear no evil:**

for thou art with me; thy rod and thy staff they comfort me. Thou preparest a table before me in the presence of mine enemies: thou anointest my head with oil; my cup runneth over. Surely goodness and mercy shall follow me all the days of my life: and I will dwell in the house of the LORD forever. He began to share what God was giving him for me through these scriptures. By the time he got to verse three, *He restoreth my soul*, I was crying and praising God because at that point I was actually "experiencing" His restoration. My peace was restored and God showed me again the blessing of a true pastor. Co-Pastor Enid Hardaway had talked to me a great deal about the importance of submitting to my ministerial covering —my pastor. It wasn't always easy because I had never walked in this realm of ministry before. God would always work things out so that I had to come back to my pastor for guidance and counseling. When I look back over these experiences, I'm thankful because I now know that everyone in the ministry must have a "godly" covering if they want to be used mightily by God. You can't just "step out" on your own without your God-given covering.

I remember that my teaching background and foundation was to always call the pastor of the church if a member called and asked me to preach. This shows respect to the church and keeps down confusion if the pastor is unaware. I was also taught never to go into a pulpit without being invited. There were times when I went to other churches with my pastor, and he always took me into their pastor's study and pulpit. I would sometimes feel that I wasn't welcome, but the pastors had too much respect for my pastor to reject me. I remember going to a church during a revival time and when we walked in, I felt something in my spirit. So I told my pastor, "I'm not going into the pulpit with you tonight. I want to sit out in the pews." His response was to encourage me to go up because we both had been to this church before and I had been welcomed. The pastor of this church was a man I had known for a while. We had studied the Word together over the years, and I had often called him my friend. When we got to the pulpit I noticed that the moderator of the Baptist Convention was there and I really wanted to turn around then and sit in the pews because I knew that he absolutely didn't favor a woman preacher. I think that I would have gone down to the pews if I had not been more concerned about how "stupid" I would have looked to the "big" crowd that was there. The moderator looked at me in disdain and frowned as I sat down. I was praying that I would be able to hold on to the end. When my friend, the pastor of this church, got up and went to the back, I joined him a few minutes later and quietly asked him if he was comfortable with me in the pulpit. He had a look of tension on his face. He said, "You can do whatever you want to do." He didn't say (as he had before) that "This is God's pulpit and you are welcome to sit here whenever you come." I knew at that moment he was wishing that I wasn't there This was devastating for me because he was my "friend." I went back out to the pulpit and fought back tears the rest of the service because the Holy Spirit didn't release me to leave out. I even had to make comments at the end with the other ministers also. My pastor encouraged me later to keep on going and not to let this hurt or hinder my journey in the ministry. This was one of many times when people I considered friends turned their backs on me in mixed company.

As God was "feeding" me and as I was "eating" from His table I discovered that the food would not always "taste" good, but was nevertheless good for me. I learned from lessons like these that just because God had called me, others wouldn't accept it. I also learned how to respond when my "friends" acted differently among different preachers. The Holy Spirit taught me to pray for strength and courage to face whatever obstacles came along. He also taught me to "forgive" even when the pain was severe. I have not perfected this, but I do see great progress. Glory, honor, and praise to my Father!!

When I look back over my ministry, after six and a half years, I thank God for all He has done for me. I started out very afraid and feeling like I must have made a mistake to accept my calling because my whole world was turned upside down. I didn't understand that this was what Jeremiah was talking about when he talked about going to the potter's house. *Jeremiah 18:1-6,* **The word which came to Jeremiah from the LORD, saying, Arise, and go down to the potter's house, and there I will cause thee to hear my words. Then I went down to the potter's house, and, behold, he wrought a work on the wheels. And the vessel that he made of clay was marred in the hand of the potter: so he made it again another vessel, as seemed good to the potter to make it. Then the word of the LORD came to me, saying, O house of Israel, cannot I do with you as this potter? saith the LORD. Behold, as the clay is in the potter's hand, so are ye in mine hand, O house of Israel.** God will make you "again" another vessel. He will continue to mold and shape you until you have become what He has "predestined" you to be. That is, if you allow Him to take you through the process.

I've seen God work mighty miracles through me from my first sermon in March of 1995 up until this present time. There were some people who came up to me after the altar call of my first sermon and said that they had been healed and that they felt burdens had been removed. Two children were saved. God has allowed and trusted me with His anointing and I don't take this blessing for granted. Every time there is a door of opportunity open for me to preach the gospel, I ask the Holy Spirit to use me mightily.

I once visited a member of my church in the hospital who had been in a coma-like state. She appeared to be alert but would just stare off into space. She hadn't spoken for more than three weeks. The Holy Spirit told me to *"go in, lay hands on her, and 'raise her from the dead'."* I had no idea of what He was telling me to do, but I went into her room somewhat afraid but willing to be obedient to my God in all things. Her brother, who was a member of the local Church of Christ, was there. I had never met him so I introduced myself, told him why I was there, and then began to pray silently for her after he agreed to allow me to pray. I laid my hands on her head and prayed quietly on the inside. After a few minutes I began to actually "feel" movement going on inside her head. Shortly after then I began to talk to her and to tell her that she had been healed. She turned to me and began to talk. I was amazed and so was her brother. I asked him if she had been talking prior to the prayer I had just prayed over her. He said she had not. I told him how awesome a healer God is. The first words this lady spoke to me were about something another lady had just said to her. The other lady she was talking about had just recently passed. She, too, had been a member of our church and they had been friends. That brought to mind what the Holy Spirit had said about *"raising"* her from the dead. She had actually been in another realm or dimension before God brought her back. I'm not sure how long she lived after this, but it was quite some time.

There was another time when the Spirit of God told me to begin praying early in the day because He had a task for me to do on this day. He said that there was someone He wanted me to pray for. I had no idea of who it was, but I did begin to pray that God would use me in whatever way He desired. It wasn't until I got a phone call later in the afternoon from a friend of mine that I realized it would be a "supernatural" task. My friend called very upset. "Linda," she said, "my husband is sick in the hospital and has been running a fever for three days. The doctors don't know what it is. Can you come and pray?" I knew right away that this was why the Holy Ghost had led me to pray earlier. I said *yes* right away. I quickly left home, and all the way from my house to the hospital room I was speaking in other tongues. I had also been fasting all day. I knew that I had to have "divine" leading to be able to accomplish this miracle.

When I came into the room, I sensed the presence of some evil spirits, but I walked up to the bed and took his hand that was swollen so badly even I couldn't believe it. He told me how he was feeling, and that the fever had not broken. The doctor did not know what had caused the swelling. I began to pray and after I left out of the room, his wife came up to me and told me that when I walked up to his bed, he started sweating and she could sense that the fever was breaking. She called back later on to say that the fever had indeed broken and that the swelling was slowly going down. He made a total recovery, thanks to God! It is so wonderful to be used as a "vessel" for the anointing. I've never understood how a person could ever even consider that they are "all that and a bag of chips" when the glory and honor belong to Almighty God.

There was one occasion when God allowed me to minister His Word and it turned out to be a greater blessing for me than for those who were present. I was asked to bring the Word at a women's retreat for one of the local churches. The message was entitled "Chosen To Be Broken," and the Holy Ghost even gave me a poem to give all of the ladies who attended this retreat at a quiet but beautiful retreat site. The poem that I wrote ended up being my own personal testimony. There were five or six women who made a life change and came forward to receive prayer to be baptized in the Holy Ghost. They asked and were ready. So God gave them all the utterance of tongues in that very hour. The poem is included in this book as an added blessing for those of you who are ready for the next step of intimacy with the Father. The Holy Spirit has used me many times "to give a Word" to people. He used me greatly in the gifts of "interpretation of tongues," "gift of the word of wisdom," and the "gift of the word of knowledge." Many times people are healed and I don't even lay my hands on them.

My Lord is Jehovah Rapha, the God that heals.

CHOSEN TO BE BROKEN

By Evangelist Linda Sweezer

What a woman you are!

What a <u>destiny</u> is planned!

No wonder you are unsure,

And have felt as if you couldn't stand.

What a woman you are!

And very soon you will see

You have been chosen by God,

To be a work of mastery.

You have been chosen, Today,

To be broken by the Potter,

And soon you'll visualize,

Why the furnace is seven times hotter.

He's breaking down His vessel,

But plans to rework each part,

Your God and Maker, great woman,

Begins his work in the heart.

You have not sinned, my sister,

Nor has He rejected your work,

He is busy, inside of you,

Healing, Healing the Hurt.

Be encouraged, don't you faint,

What you see is not a token,

You have been selected, special one,

*You have been **<u>Chosen</u> to be <u>Broken</u>.***

My advice to women who feel that God has called them into the ministry would be this:

1) Make sure you know God has called you. Prophecy should confirm "your call" and not be the "reason" you went forward. God **always** makes His will clear to us.

2) Go to your pastor before going to your church members to tell them of your call. Your pastor is your God-given covering and you should always stay in submission to him or her. Don't rush the process; your leader will then let you know the next step to take. God is a God of order. If you and your pastor don't see eye-to-eye about this issue, keep praying, but don't fight your pastor. If you are in your season, God may move you to another church where the pastor there will receive your gift. In other cases, the Lord may let you know that you "will be" going forward, but not just yet, and so stay where you are until you are released to move to this next level. The only way you will know what to do is to stay prayerful. Seek God's face about everything because all of these decisions are critical to your ministry.

3) Work in harmony with your pastor—even if you don't agree with everything he or she says or does. God taught me early on in my ministry that there were a lot of things that I "thought" I knew about ministry, but did not know. After the mistakes, I then began to really "listen" to my pastor and began to value his advice. I guess sometimes you have to "sink" before you "swim." Ministry is so "deep" that there is so much to be learned. When you look on the surface, it appears simple until you begin to move into ministry. That's when you find out how much you have to learn. One of the sad things I have seen since I have been in the ministry is preachers who take their calling "lightly." There are some who want to "pastor" a congregation even before they understand what the ministry is all about. That's why in *Isaiah 40:31:* **But they that wait upon the Lord shall renew their strength; they shall mount up with wings as eagles; they shall run, and not be weary; and they shall walk, and not faint,** God talks about the "rewards" of patience when we wait on Him. He takes us to the place where we are destined to be, and He gets us there on time. *I Timothy 1:5-7,* **Now the end of the commandment is**

charity out of a pure heart, and of a good conscience, and of faith unfeigned: From which some having swerved have turned aside unto vain jangling; Desiring to be teachers of the law; understanding neither what they say, nor whereof they affirm. When we are serious about our call to "preach" the gospel, we will totally yield and surrender ourselves to the Holy Spirit. He then will "lead and guide us into all truth." *John 16:13,* **Howbeit when He, the Spirit of truth, is come, he will guide you into all truth: for he shall not speak of himself; but whatsoever he shall hear, that shall he speak: and he will shew you things to come.** Jesus "prepared" His disciples before He sent them out. He's still preparing His servants today; those who are obedient to His voice. God will use your pastor as a way to gauge when it's time for you to go to the next level of ministry—STAY UNDER AUTHORITY!

4) Never compare yourself to other preachers with the intent of being a carbon copy of them. In *I Corinthians 12:14-18,* **For the body is not one member, but many. If the foot shall say, Because I am not the hand, I am not of the body; is it therefore not of the body? And if the**

ear shall say, Because I am not the eye, I am not of the body; is it therefore not of the body? If the whole body were an eye, where were the hearing? If the whole were hearing, where were the smelling? But now hath God set the members every one of them in the body, as it hath pleased Him, Paul talks about the diversity of each body part. So then, all are not apostles, all are not pastors, all are not evangelists or prophets. Each person is different and the call of God on their lives will not be the same. This means that God's *teaching method* will be different also. Allow God to *feed* you according to *His* course. When we "eat" what God has prepared, we turn out to be the anointed vessels we were born to become. Yes, you can reject what the Lord is giving you to *eat along the way*, but that will then render you spiritually undernourished in the areas of your calling. We don't always see the "big picture" that God has. We have to keep moving as He puts each dish down on the table before us. After a while, we will see the "big plan" and the whole meal will be laid out before us. God requires faithfulness along the way. He asks for our "trust" in Him to be greater than our confidence in our own abilities or in the abilities of others. *Proverbs 3:5-7* reads: **Trust in the LORD with all thine heart; and lean not unto thine own understanding. In all thy ways acknowledge him, and he shall direct thy paths. Be not wise in thine own eyes: fear the LORD, and depart from evil.** As a matter of fact, Pastor Forman always taught us that it's not your ability that counts; it's your availability. God has the strength and power—if we would only yield our vessels to Him. Be yourself—your preaching style is uniquely yours. Don't "practice" another person's preaching style. You will never be comfortable "pretending" to be someone else. Ask God for His wisdom in helping you to become content with who He has said you are, and move forward.

5) Study to show thyself approved, *II Timothy 2:15*, **Study to shew thyself approved unto God, a workman that needeth not to be ashamed, rightly dividing the word of truth.** Consistent prayer and study time must be in your walk with God. The Holy Spirit will take out of you only what you have put in. "NO WORD IN, NO WORD OUT!" Allow the Holy Spirit to guide your prayer time. He knows what we need to pray for, *Romans 8:26,*

Likewise the spirit also helpeth our infirmities: for we know not what we should pray for as we ought: but the spirit itself maketh intercession for us with groanings which cannot be uttered, even when we don't. Likewise, He knows what we should study on a day-to-day basis because He knows every audience we will minister to. Preachers should never study just to "preach." Because we are all Christians, we study because we want to know Him better and better. Allow the Holy Spirit to bring the revelation as you study—after all, He is the teacher.

6) To women in the ministry, don't try to "preach" about why God calls women into the ministry unless you are directly led by the Holy Ghost. The Lord showed me when He first sent me forth that if I focused on this aspect only, the devil would use it as a way of distracting me from preaching the gospel. The enemy would like for us to get mad to the degree that all of our messages seem to "men-bash" instead of "God-glorify." Stay with the Word and people will "see" why God has called you. They will see a clear picture of a messenger who is anointed and being used mightily by God to spread His

Word. After you have been preaching for a while, people will no longer look at your "gender." They will look at your "agenda." What they will see is that you love the Lord and that God's Spirit is speaking through you to them. That, my sisters, is what people really want; they want to hear from heaven. Those who never seem to hear you because of the "dress" you have on won't seem significant anymore after you have seen God's people saved, set free, filled with the Holy Ghost, and living a sanctified life, having responded to the Word that God gives you to preach. There are always "others" on this missionary journey who are waiting on that Word that God has given you.

7) Don't think that you are infallible. As anointed as you are, there will be times when what you "heard" was not the Holy Ghost. This was a very hard lesson for me to learn. When I first got filled with the Holy Ghost, my Spirit was so open to Him, and the intimacy level that the Holy Spirit took me to was so great, that I didn't realize that because I was on another level, the devil would try another "temptation." As the Holy Spirit spoke to me, so did the devil. I had never encountered principalities on this level before, so I was caught by storm. The

more God has invested in your ministry, the greater the warfare will be. I remember that during this time I was driving my car to the hospitals several times a week and praying for hours at a time outside the buildings. On one occasion, I stood right inside the door of the Emergency Room of one of the hospitals and I prayed for hours there quietly against a wall. One of the employees got tired of seeing me stand there, so she came and asked me to leave. I was so deep in the prayer that I didn't even respond to her. This was so very unlike me. I am a "follow all rules and regulations person," so I was obviously not myself this day. I stayed there even when I heard the employee say that she was going to call the police. On the inside I was about to panic and wanted to leave. But I just couldn't move. The police came, and as the officer was walking up to me to escort me out, another lady from the hospital (a nurse) who knew me well came up, realized she knew who I was, and took me by the arm to the side before the officer could do anything. I then explained to her that I was praying. The interesting thing about this was that God delivered me from a situation that the enemy was trying to control. The nurse, whom the Holy Spirit sent down at that moment, later told me that she was taking a course called Experiencing God, and that this was the type of situation they were then studying. I thought she would think I had lost my marbles. Instead, it was a demonstration to her, and another lady with whom I work, of the power and timing of God. I still feel, when I look back in retrospect, that God's will was not for me to defy the authority structure there by continuing to silently pray, but to leave quickly. Even though I missed what the Holy Spirit wanted me to do, He protected me because He knew my motive was to glorify Him and to edify His people. From this lesson I learned that the Holy Spirit will not lead us to do anything that contradicts the Word of God. *Hebrews 13:1-2,* **Let brotherly love continue. Be not forgetful to entertain strangers: for thereby some have entertained angels unawares.** Persecution, suffering, trials, and tribulation all precede the glory God reveals in His saints. If we hold on to God, He will lead us through even the toughest times. *II Timothy 3:12,* **Yea, and all that will live godly in Christ Jesus shall suffer persecution.**

When I reflect back on how God had me **Eating Along The Way!**, I can see the good and the bad, the bitter, and the sweet, and how He worked them together for my good. *Romans 8:28,* **And we know that all things work together for good to them**

that love God, to them who are the called according to his purpose.

When I was an adolescent living on Locust Street, I clearly remember a family who moved across the street from our house. They were an older couple (The Alexanders) who had a son much younger than I. Their house was a pretty, freshly-painted big white house with a giant Magnolia tree in the yard. One day as I was walking through their yard coming down the hill from the store, Mr. Alexander stopped me with great excitement in his voice. "Linda," he said, "you are the one who was in my dream. I had a dream that God called me to preach. I saw you in the dream, and I asked you how many brothers and sisters you had. You told me ten." He told me more than this, but this was the only part I could remember—even for years to come. I was speechless when he told me this. I smiled as he grabbed me and hugged me tight. "I've been called to preach, honey, and God used you to show it to me." What could I say? I left and went across the street, but I never forgot it. Reverend Alexander never let me forget it because from that day forth he called me "his girl." God had used me somehow to confirm his calling. When I reflect back on this now, I realize that the implications were deeper than I ever knew. When the Lord called me to preach, I did question why out of the ten children that my parents had—six boys and four girls—why I was the one chosen to preach—the youngest and the most insecure one. I no longer have any questions about this today because I absolutely know that I was chosen by Christ to carry His cross and His gospel message to the world.

As I was growing up, I never seemed to "fit" into any particular group. My favorite pastime was to go to my room, read, and suck my two fingers on my left hand for consolation. I didn't understand why people always said I was "different" until I understood my call to preach. Even in elementary school, God gave me teachers who did more than teach—they preached. My math teacher, Mrs. Euphytee Williams, preached to us just about every day. I didn't like it then, but I understand now that God was allowing me to *eat along the way*. I have had so many "great" teachers who truly loved the Lord. In the church where I was baptized, they always kept me busy. When I was an adolescent, God used a woman by the name of Henretta Pointer to keep me very active during this time in my life. She would call me every week and tell me what she wanted me to do. She always spoke words of encouragement to me about my skills and talents. I always thought she talked too long and did not look forward to the calls at that time. God was causing me to *eat along the way* and I truly thank Him now for her ministry.

My mother had a powerful ministry. Publicly, she was a quiet and soft-spoken woman. She never preached from a pulpit, but she **was** and *is* God's minister. Mom had a host of sick and shut-in people that she visited, ran errands for, and helped out. How in the world could a mother of ten children who was also a schoolteacher and constantly going back to update her education credentials help so many people in the community? The grace of God has always followed my mother's life. She has always been the type to give away all she has in sacrifice for others.

Mom would take me places with her where I really didn't want to go during my early years. One of the places where she often took me was the home of a very elderly lady by the name of Mrs. Taylor. It seemed to me that Mrs. Taylor spoke one word every five minutes. It took her so long to say things. I remember wanting to run out of her house just to scream because I couldn't take sitting there for hours at a time! It never seemed to bother my mother.

Her house, to me, had an elderly smell to it. I was always tuned in to the smell whenever we went there. She moved very slowly and she loved to talk. Though I was frustrated and impatient with elderly people then, God was instilling a love for the elderly in me that I would never shake off. There is something so incredible about sitting down with godly, elderly people that I don't even have words to explain what God was feeding me through my mom even during those years.

When God has a work for you to do, He begins "feeding" you at a very early age the dishes that will nourish and prepare you for His will to be done in your life. As I look back over my life, I'm thankful for what my Father has allowed me to *eat along the way*. All of His meals were "healthy" for me, even if they were not "tasty" to me. I somehow suspect that my "eating" days are not over. Although I'm walking in His fullness, there is so much more the Spirit of God wants me to eat. So I guess I'll just be **Eating Along The Way!** as He takes me to higher heights and deeper depths.

May God bless you as you are **Eating Along The Way!** of ministry. Remember, **God has not given us the Spirit of fear, but of power, love, and of a sound mind.** *II Timothy 1:7*

ABOUT THE AUTHOR

Evangelist Linda Sweezer was born the tenth child in a family of ten to Alfred and Bessie Dillard in Vicksburg, Mississippi, in 1960. She was saved at the tender age of ten years old at Mt. Zion #1 Missionary Baptist Church. She has worked at Vicksburg Family Development Service for 17 years—twelve of those years as the Co-Director with Kay Lee.

She attended Vicksburg High School and graduated from Millsaps College with a Bachelor of Arts degree in English in 1982.

Her experience as a social worker and administrator proved invaluable when God called her into the gospel ministry on February 5, 1995. She was ordained in 1997 by Reverend R.L. Forman. God has used her extensively to boldly proclaim the gospel throughout Vicksburg and surrounding areas of Mississippi.

Evangelist Sweezer is a playwright and has written, produced and directed nine major productions which were performed in the theatre and surrounding areas of Vicksburg, Rolling Fork, and Fayette, Mississippi.

Her plays include:

- One In Christ
- What Will I Be?
- Color Me Courage
- The Greatest Mystery
- Choices (Performed in Rolling Fork, Mississippi)
- What Do I Do Now? (Performed in Vicksburg and Fayette, Mississippi)
- Shattered Dreams
- Change Is Not Bad
- Double Trouble

Evangelist Sweezer has been married for 20 years to Tony Sweezer. They have two children Anthony (17 years old) and Ann (nine years old).

Her achievements include:

- Chosen by the Ivyettes of Alpha Kappa Alpha Sorority, Inc. as onc of the Religious Role Models
- Outstanding Young Women of America

- Woman of Excellence Award in Art and Literature
- Sower of the Lord Award and Peacemaker Award given by the Flying High for Jesus Outreach
- Honored as a Local Recipient of 100 Black Women

Her activities include:

- Pastor & Founder-House of Peace Worship Center, Vicksburg, MS
- Former Associate Minister, Youth Pastor, and Co-Facilitator of Women's Fellowship at Triumph Missionary Baptist Church
- Appointment by Alderwoman Gertrude Young to the Civil Service Commission for the City of Vicksburg
- Appointed by the former Mayor of Vicksburg, Robert M. Walker to the Mayor's Task Force on Race and Human Relations and the Mayor's Task Force on Domestic Violence
- Delegate to the School Choir Advisory Council.

www.ingramcontent.com/pod-product-compliance
Lightning Source LLC
Chambersburg PA
CBHW021546290526
45785CB00004BA/1760